Goldilocks and the Three Bears

RETOLD BY MARCIA LEONARD
PICTURES BY YVETTE BANEK

Silver Press

For Deborah and her three bears.
—M.L.

For my daughter, Skye.
—Y.B.

Library of Congress Cataloging-in-Publication Data
Leonard, Marcia.
    Goldilocks and the three bears / retold by Marcia Leonard; pictures by Yvette Banek.
    p. cm. — (What's missing?)
    Summary: An adaptation of the classic tale in which a tired and hungry little girl helps herself to the belongings of the three bears in the woods. At various points in the text the reader is asked to state what is missing from the picture.
    [1. Folklore. 2. Bears—Folklore. 3. Picture puzzles.]
I. Banek, Yvette Santiago, ill. II. Three bears. III. Title.
IV. Series: Leonard, Marcia. What's missing?
PZ8.1.L4238Go   1989
398.21—dc20
[E]   89-39263
ISBN 0-671-69350-6   ISBN 0-671-69346-8 (lib. bdg.)   CIP
                                                                          AC

Produced by Small Packages, Inc.
Text copyright © 1990 Small Packages, Inc.

Illustrations copyright © 1990 Small Packages, Inc.
and Yvette Banek.

All rights reserved. No part of this book may be used
or reproduced in any manner whatsoever without written
permission from the publisher.

Published by Silver Press, a division of
Silver Burdett Press, Inc.
Simon & Shuster, Inc.
Prentice Hall Bldg., Englewood Cliffs, NJ 07632.

Printed in the United States of America.

10 9 8 7 6 5 4 3 2 1

Once upon a time there were three bears who lived in a cozy cottage deep in the woods. One was a great big papa bear. One was a medium-sized mama bear. And one was a wee little baby bear.

Every morning the mama bear made a big pot of porridge for breakfast. Then she ladled it into three bowls and set them on the table to cool.

Can you see what's missing from this picture?

Is it piping hot porridge?

Is it snail and moth salad?

Is it macaroni and keys?

Or is it ink and glue stew?

While the porridge cooled, the bears always went for a walk.
But on this particular morning, they had a visitor.
Her name was Goldilocks, and she looked like a little angel.
But she was really rather naughty and spoiled,
and she had very bad manners!

Instead of knocking on the bears' front door, she just walked right in.
And instead of waiting to be invited to breakfast, she just helped herself.
First she tasted the papa bear's porridge. "Ouch!" she said. "Too hot."
Then she tasted the mama bear's porridge. "Yuck!" she said. "Too cold."
Then she tasted the baby bear's porridge. "Just right," she said,
and she ate it all up.

Goldilocks left the dirty dishes on the table and went to explore the living room. First she climbed up onto the papa bear's chair. "Too high!" she said. Then she sank down into the mama bear's chair. "Too low!" she said. Then she sat in the baby bear's chair. "Just right," she said, and she rocked and rocked and rocked.

What's missing from this picture?

Is it a prickly cactus?

Is it a giant goldfish?

Is it a rocking chair?

Or is it a bird cage?

Goldilocks rocked so hard, she broke the baby bear's chair.
She wasn't hurt—and she wasn't sorry. She just left the pieces
on the floor and went on exploring.

After she'd poked her pretty nose into every corner of the cottage, Goldilocks began to feel tired. "A nap is what I need," she said. And she went upstairs to try out the beds.

First she lay down on the papa bear's bed. "Too hard!" she said.
Then she lay down on the mama bear's bed. "Too soft!" she said.
Then she lay down on the baby bear's bed. "Just right!" she said.
And she fluffed up the pillow and closed her eyes.

What's missing now?

Is it a shiny red wagon?

Is it a wastepaper basket?

Is it a big beach blanket?

Or is it a cozy little bed?

Goldilocks fell fast asleep in the baby bear's cozy little bed.
She didn't hear the three bears come home.
"SOMEONE'S BEEN EATING MY PORRIDGE!"
the papa bear said in his great big voice.
"SOMEONE'S BEEN EATING MY PORRIDGE!"
the mama bear said in her medium-sized voice.
"SOMEONE'S BEEN EATING MY PORRIDGE!"
the baby bear said in his wee little voice.
"AND NOW IT'S ALL GONE!"

The three bears went into the living room.
"SOMEONE'S BEEN SITTING IN MY CHAIR!" the papa bear said.
"SOMEONE'S BEEN SITTING IN MY CHAIR!" the mama bear said.
"SOMEONE'S BEEN SITTING IN MY CHAIR!" the baby bear said.
"AND NOW IT'S ALL BROKEN!"

The three bears hurried upstairs to the bedroom.
"SOMEONE'S BEEN SLEEPING IN MY BED!" the papa bear said.
"SOMEONE'S BEEN SLEEPING IN MY BED!" the mama bear said.
"SOMEONE'S BEEN SLEEPING IN MY BED!" the baby bear said. "AND THERE SHE IS!"

What's missing here?

Is it a two-headed dragon?

Is it a juggling clown?

Is it a sleepy Goldilocks?

Or is it a modest moose?

Goldilocks woke up with a start. And when she saw the three bears, she let out a screech. "Help! Fire! Police!" she yelled. "There are bears in this bedroom!"

Before the bears could say a word, she hopped out of the bed and hurried down the stairs. Then she ran home as fast as her little legs could carry her—and stayed inside for a week!

Now it *may* be that Goldilocks learned something from her adventure, and that her manners improved. But as for the three bears, they were just as happy that they never saw that little girl again.